My Daily Diet: Proteins

On My Plate

On My Plate

My Daily Diet: Proteins

Celicia Scott

Mason Crest

Mason Crest
450 Parkway Drive, Suite D
Broomall, PA 19008
www.masoncrest.com

Printed and bound in the United States of America.

First printing
9 8 7 6 5 4 3 2 1

Series ISBN: 978-1-4222-3094-7
ISBN: 978-1-4222-3099-2
ebook ISBN: 978-1-4222-8790-3

Library of Congress Cataloging-in-Publication Data

Scott, Celicia, 1957- author.
  My daily diet : proteins / Celicia Scott.
      pages cm. — (On my plate)
  Audience: Age 9+
  Audience: Grade 4 to 6.
  Includes bibliographical references and index.
  ISBN 978-1-4222-3099-2 (hardback) — ISBN 978-1-4222-3094-7 (series) — ISBN 978-1-
4222-8790-3 (ebook) 1. Proteins in human nutrition—Juvenile literature. 2. Proteins—Juvenile
literature. I. Title.
  TX553.P7S39 2015
  612.3'98—dc 3
                                    2014010567

Contents

KEY ICONS TO LOOK FOR:

 Text-Dependent Questions: These questions send the reader back to the text for more careful attention to the evidence presented there.

 Words to Understand: These words with their easy-to-understand definitions will increase the reader's understanding of the text, while building vocabulary skills.

 Series Glossary of Key Terms: This back-of-the book glossary contains terminology used throughout this series. Words found here increase the reader's ability to read and comprehend higher-level books and articles in this field.

 Research Projects: Readers are pointed toward areas of further inquiry connected to each chapter. Suggestions are provided for projects that encourage deeper research and analysis.

 Sidebars: This boxed material within the main text allows readers to build knowledge, gain insights, explore possibilities, and broaden their perspectives by weaving together additional information to provide realistic and holistic perspectives.

Introduction

Most of us would agree that building healthy bodies and minds is a critical component of future success in school, work, and life. Providing our bodies with adequate and healthy nutrition in childhood sets the stage for both optimal learning and healthy habits in adulthood. Research suggests that the epidemic of overweight and obesity in young children leads to a large medical and financial burden, both for individuals and society. Children who are overweight and obese are more likely to become overweight or obese adults, and they are also at increased risk for a range of diseases.

Developing healthy eating and fitness habits in childhood is one of the most important gifts we can all provide to children in our homes and workplaces—but as any parent can attest, this is not always an easy task! Children are surrounded with both healthy and unhealthy eating options in their homes, schools, and in every restaurant or store they visit. Glossy marketing of food and meals is ubiquitous in media of all types, impacting both children's and adults' eating choices. As a result of the multiple influences on eating choices, from infancy through adulthood, we all benefit from additional support in making healthy choices.

Just as eating and fitness can become habits in adulthood, personal decision-making in childhood is critical to developing healthy habits. Providing healthy options and examples are a starting point, which can support children's healthy habits, but children also benefit from understanding the rationale for eating reasonable portions of healthy foods. Parents, teachers, and others often communicate messages through their words and actions—but books can provide more detailed information and pictures.

Building on this need for developing informed consumers, the ON MY PLATE series provides elementary school children with an informative yet fun introduction to their eating options. Beginning with an introduction to the five food groups, children can learn about what they ideally will have on their own plate and in their mouths. Tips are provided for choosing healthy snacks. And children will understand the importance of eating a range of foods. These books empower our children to make healthy decisions for themselves.

An additional benefit of this series may be the trickle-up effect for parents. Even if we all *know* the importance of making healthy choices for meals and snacks, there's nothing like a child *reminding us* why this is important. When our children start citing the long-term consequences of our dietary choices, we tend to listen!

Here's to developing healthy eating habits today!

Lisa Albers Prock, MD, MPH
Developmental Behavioral Pediatrician, Boston Children's Hospital
Assistant Professor, Harvard Medical School

WORDS TO UNDERSTAND

conveyer belts: Moving bands of fabric or rubber that carry things from one place to another.

efficiently: In an effective manner, without wasting anything.

slaughtered: Killed for food.

tofu: A protein-rich food made from mashed soybeans.

Chapter 1

Where Does Protein Come From?

Meat, beans, fish, *tofu*—these foods may seem to have little in common. But in fact, they share something very important. They all contain protein.

Protein is a nutrient. Nutrients are found in foods and help the body work correctly and *efficiently*. Our bodies need more protein than they do other nutrients. Protein keeps muscles working right. Protein is what muscles, organs, and the immune system are made of. Without protein, your body can't be healthy.

Protein foods come from animals and plants. These foods include chicken, fish, eggs, nuts, beans, seeds, beef, pork, and tofu. Some protein foods come from animals and some come from plants.

ANIMAL PROTEINS

Animals are the source of many protein foods. Meat (including beef, pork, goat, chicken, turkey, and seafood) was once a living animal. And because those animals were made up of protein, the meat they provide also has protein.

Animals from farms usually go to a special slaughterhouse, then are butchered for meat. This meat is then shipped to your grocery store.

MAKE CONNECTIONS

Not everyone is so happy about factory farms. Some people don't like how factor farms treat animals or the methods used to slaughter them. Many people are worried about the health problems factory farms may cause for animals, people, and the Earth. Factory farms keep animals so close together, they often get sick. And because the animals are packed into a limited space, disease and illness can spread quickly. Then they are given medicines called antibiotics to keep them healthy, but those antibiotics may be harmful for people who later eat meat from those animals. So many animals together also means a lot of animal waste, which pollutes the land and water around the farm. Luckily, there are alternatives for people who don't want to eat meat from factory farms. Smaller farmers often keep only a few animals and give them lots of space. They treat the animals better, and they are healthier for people and the environment. These farms sometimes sell their meat right on site or at farmers' markets. More and more grocery stores provide such meats as options for their customers.

Most of the meat we eat comes from farms. Farmers provide their meat animals with food, water, and shelter. Most animals raised for food are **slaughtered** when the animals are big enough to eat, sometimes when they are just a few months old.

Today, animal farms are often more like factories and are actually referred to as "factory farms." Many animals are housed close together, with little room to move. This way, people who run the farms can make more money and use less space. In some cases, animals are raised on fields and then sent to factory farms to fatten up for their last few weeks or months.

There are even fish farms! Fish farmers keep giant tanks (more like pools) full of fish, which they feed and watch over. Other farmers farm fish right in the ocean. They create cages or roped-off areas in the ocean to raise shellfish, like shrimp and clams.

Some fish are caught in the wild rather than farmed. Fishermen and fisherwomen go out on the ocean in boats, and use big nets to catch fish. Lobstermen and lobsterwomen use cages to trap lobsters and then haul them on board.

Other animal protein foods include eggs. Eggs aren't meat, but they do come from birds. Most commonly, you'll find chicken eggs in the grocery store, but people can eat all sorts of eggs—even ostrich!

Farms also raise chickens for eggs. In today's world, thousands of chickens are often kept in one place. They often sit in cages and lay eggs that roll out onto **conveyer belts**.

BUTCHERING AND PACKAGING

Once the animals are slaughtered, they have to be butchered. That means they have to be skinned or defeathered, sliced into cuts of meat, and packaged to sell in grocery stores.

The steak, ground beef, drumsticks, and sausage you see in the store all came from a

RESEARCH PROJECT

Not every plant grows in every place in the world. The text gives several examples of plants that provide protein. Use the Internet to research where some of these plants grow. Choose one nut, one seed, and one type of bean. You may choose the examples given in the text or come up with your own examples. What conditions do these plants need to grow? Which countries grow them the most? Do any of them grow where you live? If so, do some additional research to find out if there is a farm near you that grows the plant.

whole animal. Someone cut the animal into pieces to sell. For example, a chicken is cut into drumsticks, thighs, wings, and breasts. Even the giblets (organs like the heart and liver) are saved and packaged. Many people eat them or use them to make gravy.

You'll find the cuts of meat packaged in the grocery store. You don't usually see an entire cow or pig in the store! Even the whole chickens you can buy don't have heads, feet, or feathers.

Not every part of the animal can be eaten. Any part that can't be served as food, like a chicken's head and feathers, is usually removed before it is sold.

TEXT-DEPENDENT QUESTIONS

1. What are the two main sources of protein?

2. Describe two ways people farm fish.

3. According to the sidebar, some people don't like to eat meat from factory farms. What are some of the reasons they give?

4. What are the five steps farmers use to grow plant protein foods?

5. Define what a processed food is, and give two examples.

PLANT PROTEINS

Animals aren't the only source of protein. Plant sources include nuts, seeds, and beans. All those grow on farms around the world. Among protein-bearing plants are soybeans, peanuts, black beans, chickpeas, sunflower seeds, and almonds.

No matter what kind of plant, the farmer and farmworkers prepare the soil, plant seeds, water, and sometimes add fertilizer to help the plants grow. For many plant protein foods, farmers have to plant new seeds every year. However, for nuts, a farmer plants a tree once and then waits a few years before the nuts are ready to harvest.

When the nuts, seeds, or beans are ready to harvest, the farmer and farmworkers pick them. On big farms, they use a machine. On small farms, the farmer might pick everything by hand.

PROCESSING AND PACKAGING

Plant protein foods aren't quite ready to be eaten yet. First, the nuts, seeds, or beans have to be dried out, or they will get moldy. They are left out to dry or sometimes baked in ovens to dry them out. Sometimes they are dried at the farm and sometimes at factories.

Some of them are then made into other foods at factories. For example, peanuts are ground up and mixed with salt to make peanut butter. Fresh (not dried) soybeans are pressed so all the liquid inside comes out. What's left is pressed into blocks and turned into tofu. These foods are called processed foods.

Once foods are processed, they have to be packaged. Factories put them into containers and send them to grocery stores, where people like you can buy them!

WORDS TO UNDERSTAND

bacteria: Tiny organisms too small to see. Some bacteria can make you sick, but others help to keep your healthy!

carbohydrates: The main kind of molecule our body uses for energy. Carbohydrates can be simple, like in sugar, or complex, like in bread and pasta.

consequences: The results of something. They're often negative.

digestive system: The parts of your body that work together to break down food.

nervous system: The cells that carry messages from your brain to your body and back again.

viruses: Like bacteria, viruses are too small to see, and they can make you sick—but they aren't really alive.

Chapter 2

Why Do I Need to Eat Protein Every Day?

Protein, like all nutrients, keeps the body healthy and strong, so you need to eat it every day. Not having enough protein in your diet can have serious *consequences*. Understanding some protein science sheds light on why protein is so important for good health.

WHAT DOES PROTEIN DO?

One of the main functions of protein is to build tissues in your body. Tissues are the structures your body is made of. You have muscle tissue, bone tissue, liver tissue, and more.

Your body uses protein to build muscles and keep you healthy. If you're going to be active, it's especially important to get enough protein.

Your tissues are made of protein. And when those tissues get injured, protein helps repair and replace them. For example, if you bruise a muscle or sprain an ankle, protein is there to get your body working again the way it should.

Every cell in your body contains protein. It builds your heart, muscles, and parts of your red blood cells. So without protein, you wouldn't even be here!

MAKE CONNECTIONS

After you eat protein foods, your digestive system breaks them down into amino acids. Then your body uses the protein in the form of amino acids. The human body can actually make some amino acids. But there are 9 it can't make, and the body has to get these through food. Protein from animal sources has all 9 amino acids, while protein from plant sources does not. Vegetarians (people who don't eat meat) have to be sure to get all the amino acids they need by eating lots of different plant proteins. If they do, they can get all necessary amino acids. For example, eating rice and beans or peanut butter and whole-wheat bread will provide all the needed amino acids.

Protein also forms something called antibodies. The immune system uses antibodies to attack invading **bacteria** and **viruses** in the body. Antibodies keep you from getting sick.

Protein also gives you energy. Three kinds of nutrients provide energy—fat, **carbohydrates**, and protein. Without energy, you wouldn't be able to do anything. You couldn't walk, write, play sports, or even breathe or pump blood!

Protein provides energy in the form of calories. A calorie is a measure of how much energy a food has. Twenty calories isn't very much energy. Two hundred calories provides a good amount of energy. And 2,000 calories is a lot! In fact, most people need to eat around 2,000 calories every day, though it depends on how active you are, how old you are, and whether you are a girl or a boy.

One gram of protein contains 4 calories. So a 6-ounce piece of meat contains 24 calories from protein. The meat actually has many more calories. They come from other sources, like fat. Your body then uses the energy from protein to do all sorts of daily things.

OTHER NUTRIENTS IN PROTEIN FOODS

Protein foods don't just have protein in them. They also have many other nutrients that help keep you healthy. When you eat protein foods, you get them too, along with protein.

Protein foods tend to have a lot of vitamin B. There are actually several varieties of vitamin B, and protein foods contain a wide range of them. Vitamin B helps the body release energy for you to use, keeps the **nervous system** working right, and helps create red blood cells.

Many protein foods are also high in iron. The blood uses iron to carry oxygen around your body. Without enough oxygen, you feel tired and sluggish. So without iron, you would feel tired all the time.

Lots of people think that meat is the best place to get protein, but you can also get protein from a lot of different plant foods—like beans or soy.

RESEARCH PROJECT

The text mentions the two other kinds of nutrients that provide people with energy—fats and carbohydrates. Research these other nutrients. Write a few paragraphs about each one, answering the following questions: How does the nutrient keep your body healthy? What are the different types of each nutrient? What are some good sources of the nutrient? How much of the nutrient should you eat every day? Can the nutrient cause health problems? If so, how?

TEXT-DEPENDENT QUESTIONS

1. What structure in the body does protein repair?

2. What are calories? How does protein relate to calories?

3. About how many calories do most people need to eat every day?

4. Name two other nutrients that protein foods tend to have in them.

5. How does iron keep you feeling energetic?

Fat is another nutrient often found in protein foods. People need to eat fat, because it helps protect the body's organs, keeps cells working right, and provides energy. Some fats are less healthy, especially fat found in animal protein foods. That sort of fat is called saturated fat. Healthier fats are found in plant protein foods, like nuts. Healthier fat is called unsaturated fat.

So while protein is important, so are the nutrients that hitch a ride with that protein. When you eat protein foods, you're also getting a lot of other nutritious benefits as well.

WORDS TO UNDERSTAND

context: The words before and after another word, that help you understand its meaning.

Chapter

3

So Why Can't I Just Eat Protein Every Day?

f protein is so healthy, why can't you just eat protein foods every day? Protein is just one important nutrient that you need to eat every day. Other foods have plenty of other nutrients you don't get from protein foods. Eating a variety of healthy foods is the best way to have a healthy diet.

FOOD GROUPS

To make eating healthier easier, the U.S. Department of Agriculture (USDA) divided food into five food groups. One food group is the protein foods and includes meat, beans, and nuts. The other four groups are fruit, vegetables, grains, and dairy.

Each food group contains foods with a different arrangement of nutrients. Fruits and vegetables, for example, have a lot of micronutrients—the vitamins and minerals people need in small amounts to stay healthy. Citrus fruits are high in vitamin C. Dark leafy greens, like spinach, have a lot of iron, and carrots have lots of vitamin B.

Grains have lots of good nutrients in them as well. Rice, wheat, and oats are all grains.

Junk foods like chips don't have many nutrients in them. Nutritionists often call these "empty calories" and don't consider them to be part of any food group.

MAKE CONNECTIONS

Vitamins and minerals are both types of nutrients necessary for good health. They come from different sources, though. Vitamins are named A through K and made by plants. People need to eat those plants (or the animals that eat them) to get those nutrients, since our bodies can't make them. Minerals are similar, but plants don't make them. They come from the ground. Plants suck minerals up from the soil, and when we eat those plants, we get the minerals. Vitamins and minerals are all part of a long food chain!

They are the seeds of certain plants, which can be ground into flour and made into other foods, like bread and pasta. Grains have carbohydrates, some protein, vitamins, and minerals.

Dairy is food made from animal milk. Cheese, yogurt, and milk itself are all dairy foods. They are high in fats, calcium, and iron. They also contain some protein.

You'll notice there are some foods that aren't in a food group. Junk foods and drinks—like soda, chips, candy, and some baked goods—are not part of a food group. They aren't really part of a healthy diet, although you can indulge in them occasionally and still have a healthy diet. Chips, for example, are usually made out of potatoes. But they aren't part of the vegetable group. The nutritious benefits of potatoes are offset by the fact that chips are deep-fried and have a lot of salt in them. Don't turn to junk food to cover your food groups!

A BALANCED DIET

Food groups make it easier to figure out how to eat a balanced diet. A balanced diet means eating food from every food group to get all the nutrients in each group. Balanced diets tend to equal healthy diets.

MAKE CONNECTIONS

People with food allergies and intolerances sometimes can't eat an entire food group. For example, some people are lactose intolerant, which means their bodies can't digest dairy foods. They can still have a balanced diet, though, if they pay a little more attention to what they eat. While a lactose-intolerant person can't eat dairy, he can eat more foods with the nutrients he's missing by not drinking milk or eating cheese. To get the calcium he's missing, he can eat more spinach, kale, collard greens, beans, and fish. Not eating a food group doesn't automatically mean you'll have an unbalanced diet, but you will have to put in more effort to make sure you stay healthy.

Eating a balanced diet means eating lots of different foods. Vegetables are important because lots of people don't eat them enough—but a salad like this won't give you the protein you need!

TEXT-DEPENDENT QUESTIONS

1. What are the 5 food groups?

2. List 3 nutrients dairy foods are high in.

3. Based on the first sidebar in this chapter, what is the difference between vitamins and minerals?

4. How do you define a balanced diet? What would a balanced diet look like?

5. Why do you need to eat all 5 food groups every day?

In this **context**, the word "diet" means the kind of food and how much food a person eats. It doesn't mean eating only certain things or limiting how much you eat so you can lose weight. Someone with a vegetarian diet doesn't eat meat. Someone with an unhealthy diet may eat only junk food or eat too much. A person with a balanced diet gets a good amount of nutrients from each of the food groups.

So while protein is a great addition to your diet, it isn't the only food group you should be eating. If you only ate chicken every day, you would get a lot of protein. You'd also get some fat, iron, and vitamin B—all good things.

But what about all those other nutrients you'd miss out on? You need to add all the other vitamins and minerals. You also need to eat carbohydrates (including sugar, fiber, and starch). For that, you turn to the other food groups.

RESEARCH PROJECT

Not all countries define food groups in the same way. People in various cultures and countries eat differently from the suggested five food groups. For example, in Singapore, there are four food groups, called rice and alternatives, fruit, vegetables, and meat and alternatives. People in Singapore (and many Asians in general) tend not to be able to digest dairy foods, so dairy is only listed as a meat alternative, rather than a whole food group by itself. Choose a country and do some research online into how that country defines its food groups. You may find information based on other countries' food pyramids (which you'll learn more about in the next chapter). Also do some research about why that country's food groups look different from the model you already know. Write a paragraph or two about what the other country's food groups are and why they are organized that way.

Chapter 4

Putting Protein on My Plate Every Day

Knowing you should eat protein foods every day is one thing. Figuring out how to do it is another. Fortunately, the USDA has a tool–MyPlate–that makes it easier. MyPlate helps you figure out which foods count as protein foods (and other food groups), how much you should eat, and how to eat more protein.

USING MYPLATE

MyPlate looks like it sounds–a plate. It is a picture of a plate divided into four sections. One half is divided in half again, a purple protein section and an orange grain section. The other half is divided into a smaller red fruit section and a larger green vegetable section. Off in the upper right-hand corner is a blue glass, representing dairy.

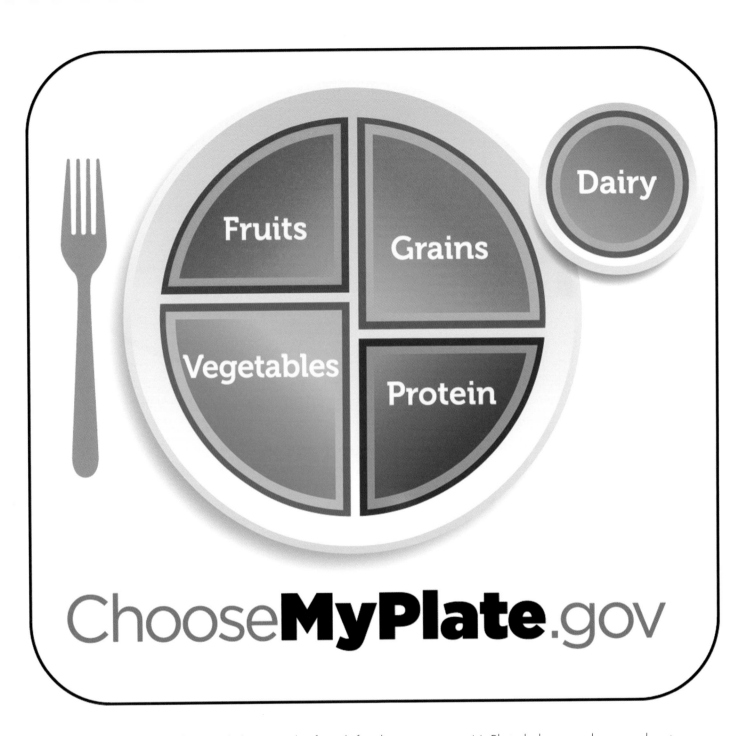

ChooseMyPlate.gov

Instead of telling people exactly how much of each food group to eat, MyPlate helps people remember to eat a little of everything in the right amounts. For example, you should eat a little bit more vegetables and grains than fruits and protein.

The picture tells you how much of each food group you should eat every day. If you were going to apply it to one meal, you would want each food to fit into its food group section. You might be eating a burrito, a fruit salad, and drinking a glass of milk. If you separated out all the ingredients in your burrito, you could place all the grains (tortilla,

MAKE CONNECTIONS

If you get most of your protein from meat, you should consider choosing leaner portions. Lean meat has less fat in it. Some fat is healthy, and you need it to be healthy. But too much fat, especially the unhealthy fats called saturated fats, can lead to health problems. To avoid that, eat lean meats like roasts, pork loin, ham, and chicken. If you eat ground beef, choose the package that says at least "90% lean." If you end up with meat with a lot of fat on it, you can trim it off. And drain any fat that drips off when the meat is cooking.

rice) in the grain section, all the protein (beans, meat) into the protein section, and all the vegetables (peppers, onions, tomatoes) in the vegetable section. Then you would place the fruit salad in the fruit section and the glass of milk in the dairy section.

Another way to understand using MyPlate is to think about the food you eat over an entire day. Not every meal you eat is going to have all five food groups. Imagine all the food you eat over the whole day fitting on a giant plate. The amounts you eat of each food group should fit into each section on the huge plate.

By following MyPlate, you're making sure you're eating a balanced diet. You're eating all five food groups, and you're eating the right amounts of each to get the nutrients you need. If you ate mostly fruit every day, with a tiny bit of each of the other food groups, you wouldn't have a very balanced diet.

HOW MUCH?

The MyPlate website also gives guidelines about how much of each food group to eat. For protein, some people need more than others. Kids tend to need to eat fewer protein foods than young and middle-aged adults. Men tend to need more protein than women. Also, the more active a person is, the more protein he or she needs. Here are the guidelines:

- Children 2–3 years old: 2 ounces
- Children 4–8 years old: 4 ounces
- Girls 9–13 years old: 5 ounces
- Boys 9–13 years old: 5 ounces
- Girls 14–18 years old: 5 ounces
- Boys 14–18 years old: 6.5 ounces
- Women 19–30 years old: 5.5 ounces
- Men 19–30 years old: 6.5 ounces
- Women 31–50 years old: 5 ounces
- Men 31–50 years old: 6 ounces

- Women 51+ years old: 5 ounces
- Men 51+ years old: 5.5 ounces

But what does an ounce of protein look like? It depends on what kind of protein food it is. One ounce of protein is equal to:

- ¼ cup of cooked beans
- 1 egg
- 1 tablespoon of peanut butter
- 1 small hamburger
- 1 sandwich slice of meat
- 12 almonds
- ¼ cup tofu
- 1 cup bean or lentil soup
- 2 tablespoons hummus

Now you just need to match your age and sex with the protein foods you like to eat. If you are a nine-year-old girl, you need to eat 5 ounces of protein. You could eat 2 tablespoons of peanut butter with breakfast, a sandwich with 2 slices of turkey for lunch, and a cup of lentil soup for dinner. If you are a fifteen-year-old boy, you'd need to eat all that plus another half tablespoon of peanut butter and another slice of turkey to get up to 6.5 ounces.

ADDING MORE PROTEIN TO YOUR DAY

Not everyone gets enough protein every day. If you're looking for ways to sneak some more protein into your diet, there are plenty of tricks.

Mix up your choices so that you get all the nutrition from each sort of protein food. Lots of people only think of meat when they think of protein. Even if your favorite protein food is meat, eat a variety of meats. Don't just stick with hamburgers all the time. Try

RESEARCH PROJECT

Do some research online on the nutrients found in three protein foods of your choice. Pick at least one nonmeat protein food. Make sure you're finding information about equivalent amounts of food. So if you find nutrition information for 1 ounce of steak, make sure you're also finding the equivalent nutrition information for, say, 2 tablespoons of peanut butter. Write down the amounts of protein and fat and as many vitamins and minerals you can find for each one. Then compare the amounts of nutrients in each. Which source has the most protein? Which has the most vitamin A? How about iron?

TEXT-DEPENDENT QUESTIONS

1. What is MyPlate meant to be used for?

2. How many sections does MyPlate have? What do these sections correspond to?

3. How much protein would a 17-year-old boy need to eat? What about a 38-year-old woman?

4. Name 3 equivalent amounts of food that equal 1 ounce of protein.

6. According to the sidebar, why should you choose to eat lean meats?

ground turkey or fish. Beans in burritos, soups, and salads are also a great choice and add variety to your protein choices.

Stick more protein in your sandwiches. Try lunch meat, hummus, or peanut butter and jelly. Add protein to salads with nuts, chicken, or tofu.

Try to eat protein with every meal or almost every meal. You can sneak in some protein with snacks or when eating fast food.

Chapter 5

Fast Foods, Snacks, and Protein

You can eat protein just about anywhere. Eat it at home, at school, and at restaurants. You can even eat protein as a part of fast-food meals and snacks.

FAST FOOD

Many menu items found at fast-food restaurants are actually full of protein. But not all that protein is as healthy as it could be. The trick to healthy is to find the best protein options.

Walk into a burger joint, and you'll see hamburgers, cheeseburgers, chicken nuggets and fingers, and fried-fish sandwiches. All of them are protein foods. But are they the best choices for protein foods?

The way to choose the right protein foods in fast-food restaurants is to think about fat and calories. A lot of those foods are really high in unhealthy fats. It's better to choose lean meats with less fat.

Fast food usually gives you plenty of protein—but it also has a lot of fat and sugar, and usually not enough of certain nutrients like vitamins.

Much fast food is unhealthy, because it has a lot of calories. Remember, calories are how we measure the energy in food. Healthier foods, like fruits and vegetables, tend to have fewer calories. One apple may only have 100 calories. Less-healthy foods tend to have a lot of calories. One fast-food hamburger could have 600 calories. Some of the most extreme hamburgers might even have 1,000 calories or more!

Most people need to eat between 1,800 and 2,200 calories per day. Calories are a good thing, not a bad thing, because we need calories of energy to live. Without energy, we wouldn't be able to do anything. But eating too many calories every day leads to weight gain and health problems.

If you eat one of those 1,000-calorie hamburgers, you're eating about one-third of all the calories you need for an entire day. A single food that provides that many calories is not very healthy for you. Fortunately, there are plenty of healthier choices at fast-food restaurants.

If you go out to eat at a fast-food restaurant, look for the healthy protein options. Burgers and chicken sandwiches can be good choices, as long as they don't have a lot of extra stuff on them. Staying away from mayonnaise and bacon are good ways of keeping down the fat and calories while getting some protein.

Go for baked or grilled meats rather than fried. So if you order a chicken sandwich or a salad, get the baked or grilled chicken option.

There aren't quite as many nonmeat protein options at fast-food restaurants. If you look hard though, you can find a few. For example, if you're at a Mexican fast-food place, you can order beans. If tofu or nuts are options for your salad, go for those. For breakfast, you can order oatmeal with nuts or egg sandwiches. While fast food probably won't ever be completely healthy, you can keep an eye on your health by ordering some protein.

SNACKS

Snacks are another way to get more protein into your diet. Snacks are a great way to keep up your energy during the day. If you have hours and hours between breakfast and lunch and you get hungry halfway through, have a snack.

Snacks are great for getting more food groups into your diet. If you haven't gotten enough of one food group during your regular meals, you can always choose a snack from that food group. For example, if you haven't eaten any protein foods all day, and you know you're going to be eating pizza for dinner (which doesn't have very much protein in it), you can have a protein snack.

Here are a few choices for protein snacks. You can choose snacks with or without meat in them, but all have a healthy dose of protein for your day.

- A handful or two of mixed nuts or trail mix, with nuts of your choice, sunflower seeds, and other things, like coconut flakes, and dried fruits. You can even add a little chocolate.
- Roasted pumpkin or squash seeds, especially unsalted, are good choices.
- Celery sticks with peanut butter smeared in the middle. Add some raisins on top to make this snack into "ants on a log."
- Hummus and veggies or pita cut into triangles. Hummus is a dip made out of chickpeas and sesame seed paste called tahini.
- Edamame, which is the Japanese word for fresh soybeans. You can buy them fresh or frozen. It's fun to pop out the soybeans from their pods.

Mixing food groups is a great way to make sure you're getting a balanced diet. This snack has protein from the peanut butter, but also vegetables and fruits from the celery and raisins.

- Add peanut, almond, or sunflower butter to a piece of whole-grain toast.
- Mix nuts and fruit into yogurt.
- Fold a tortilla in half, and put cheese and beans in the middle. Melt the cheese in the microwave or on the stovetop.
- Make a peanut butter smoothie with bananas, yogurt, and milk or juice.

RESEARCH PROJECT

Do some research into your favorite fast-food meals. Pick a restaurant and a meal from that restaurant that you've eaten before. Check online for nutrition information for each of the foods in that meal. For example, you might find information on a Happy Meal with a cheeseburger, french fries, and milk. Write down the calories for the meal, along with the amount of fat and protein. Can you find another meal that is slightly healthier?

TEXT-DEPENDENT QUESTIONS

1. What are the two ways fast-food protein can be unhealthy?

2. What do calories measure?

3. How many calories should you eat every day?

4. List three fast-food protein meals, including one nonmeat option.

5. Why is it important to eat snacks during the day?

- A hard-boiled egg can be eaten whole. Or chop, add whole-grain mustard, and serve with vegetables or on whole-wheat crackers.
- Deli meat or tuna on whole-wheat crackers is another good option.

Be creative, and make up your own snacks. Pick your favorite protein and make a little meal out of it to keep yourself going between real meals.

WORDS TO UNDERSTAND

circulatory system: Your blood vessels and heart, which work together to bring oxygen and nutrients to your body and carry wastes away.

strokes: Blocked or burst blood vessels in your brain.

Chapter
6

The Big Picture

So why is all this healthy eating stuff important anyway? Healthy eating is important because it makes a big positive difference in your life. You'll feel better and may even avoid some serious health problems if you choose to eat healthfully.

HEALTHY EATING AND ENERGY

One important reason to eat healthy is your energy. You've noticed the difference between feeling energized and ready to go and feeling sluggish and lazy. Healthy eating can help you feel more like the first and less like the second.

Eating nutritious food gives you steady energy that keeps you going for longer periods of time. You'll be able to pay attention in school, play soccer or whatever sport you like, go to dance or music lessons, and still have energy to hang out with friends and family.

Sugar might make you feel energized and awake for a little while—but soon it will wear off and you'll "crash." Eating a balanced diet can help you have a steady amount of energy all day.

MAKE CONNECTIONS

With all this talk of healthy food, it's easy to overlook the second important component of staying healthy—exercise. Human bodies are made to move, and moving around keeps them working right. Today, many people end up not moving much. Instead, they sit around too much. Don't park yourself in front of the TV or computer. Get up and move! Choose activities you like to do. Join a sports team, go walking or hiking, play a game with your friends at school or in the park, take a dance or martial arts class. The list is endless. Regular exercise helps you maintain a healthy weight and prevents all sorts of health problems, just like healthy eating.

Unhealthy foods do the opposite. Take sugar, for example. When you eat a lot of sugar all at once, you might feel a burst of energy. Sugar gives you a rush of energy that makes you want to run around. First of all, that might not be the kind of energy you need. If you have to sit in school for a few hours, you don't want the urge to run around and fidget. You want to be able to pay attention and learn. Sugar won't give you that!

After your burst of energy from sugar, there's an energy crash. You'll feel tired and worn-out. You might even have a headache. These things aren't great for school or anywhere you need to pay attention.

HEALTHY EATING AND WEIGHT

Another reason healthy eating is important is your weight. Your weight can tell you how healthy you are. Healthy weight does not mean everyone has to be extremely thin. In fact, for some people, being extremely thin is very unhealthy.

Everyone has a different healthy weight. Some people's bodies are meant to weigh more when they're healthy, and some are meant to weigh less. It doesn't have anything to do with how beautiful, smart, or worthwhile someone is.

The important thing is to figure out your own healthy weight. When a body is at its healthy weight, it works correctly. It lets you run around and do everything you want to do without breaking down. (Of course, you might still twist an ankle or break a bone at your healthy weight. That's a different story.) You also feel good when you're at a healthy weight.

Bodies that weigh too much or too little don't work as well as they could. Weighing too much can lead to bone and joint problems and difficulty moving around. It can also lead to serious health problems, like diabetes, heart attacks, and *strokes*. On the other hand, weighing too little can make it hard to have enough energy to do everything you need or want to do in a day.

MAKE CONNECTIONS

Nutritionists talk about two categories of people who weigh too much. People who are overweight weigh a little more than is healthy. People who are obese weigh a lot more than is healthy. Nutritionists use a number called the body mass index (BMI) to figure out if someone is overweight or obese. The BMI is based on age, weight, and height. People with healthy weights have BMIs of 18.5 to 24.9. Overweight people have BMIs of 25 to 29.9. Anyone with a BMI over 30 is considered obese.

Eating healthfully can lead directly to a healthy weight. When you eat a variety of healthy foods, in the correct amounts, you keep your weight down. Weight has a lot to do with calories especially. People who eat too many calories every day will start to gain weight. People who eat too few calories every day will be too underweight. Eating just the right amount of calories gives your body all the energy it needs and keeps you at a healthy weight.

HEALTHY EATING AND DISEASE

Eating healthy foods also helps prevent diseases today and in the future. People can face many health problems because of a poor diet. Luckily, a lot of these problems can be prevented by choosing to eat healthier. While healthy eating isn't magic, and won't keep you from ever getting sick, it can reduce the risk for getting serious diseases.

Diabetes is a major disease that, in some cases, can be prevented by following a healthy diet. Diabetes occurs when the body can't process sugar the way it should. The body makes a substance called insulin. Insulin changes the sugar you eat into energy the body can use or store. The bodies of people with type 1 diabetes don't make any insulin. Type 1 diabetes doesn't have much to do with unhealthy eating. However, type 2 diabetes does. With type 2 diabetes, the body doesn't respond correctly to the insulin it makes. Unhealthy diets and lack of exercise can lead to type 2 diabetes.

And diabetes can lead to even more health problems, like heart disease, liver and kidney disease, eye problems, foot problems, and more. Sometimes, diabetes can be managed by eating better. But sometimes shots and pills are also needed.

Other serious diet-related diseases include heart disease and stroke. Diets high in certain nutrients—like fat, cholesterol, and sodium—can lead to these heart problems. Healthy eating goes a long way toward keeping your heart and *circulatory system* healthy.

Sometimes it's hard to want to eat healthfully because of what might happen in the future. So think about how eating healthy can help you today.

Besides feeling energetic and awake and maintaining a good weight, healthy eating

Remember, eating healthy isn't about getting a lot of any one kind of food. It's about eating many different foods, and getting a little bit of what you need from each of them.

RESEARCH PROJECT

This chapter includes some numbers about diabetes. When people do studies to answer questions about groups of people, the answers to their questions are usually numbers—the number of people that have a certain disease, for example, or the the percentage, which refers to how many people in a group of 100 have that disease. All these numbers are called statistics. Research another diet-related disease and find some statistics about it. You may choose heart disease, colon cancer, osteoporosis, stroke, liver disease, or another condition. Write a paragraph about how the disease you chose is related to diet. Write another about the statistics associated with that disease, such as how many people are diagnosed with it each year and how many die.

MAKE CONNECTIONS

Many people have diabetes. As of 2013, almost 26 million people in the United States have type 2 diabetes. That's almost 8.5 percent of the entire population! That number includes 215,000 people under the age of 20. Type 2 diabetes isn't just something that affects older people.

helps boost your immune system. A strong immune system is better able to fight off invading bacteria and viruses and will keep you feeling well, instead of getting sick all the time. People who eat healthier tend to have stronger immune systems and get sick less often.

Cutting out unhealthy junk food from your diet may also prevent some unpleasant side effects. Choosing healthy foods with fiber and other good nutrients keeps your digestive tract working better. You can prevent stomachaches and gas. Unhealthy eating can also cause headaches and other kinds of unpleasant feelings. Making healthy food choices can cut down on all those experiences and keep you strong and able to do everything you love to do!

Protein and other healthy nutrients are essential to a healthy life. Without protein, your muscles, organs, immune system, and more suffer. From animal proteins like meat and eggs, to plant proteins like nuts and beans, protein foods are an important part of a healthy diet.

Protein is just one piece of the puzzle. Adding in all the necessary nutrients and all the food groups will benefit you immediately and in the future. You'll never look back!

TEXT-DEPENDENT QUESTIONS

1. Describe what eating a lot of sugar does to your energy levels.

2. Why is having a healthy weight important?

3. According to the first sidebar, what is the other important part of staying healthy besides eating well?

4. What are 3 health problems diabetes can lead to?

5. Name 2 ways healthy eating will help you feel good right away.

Find Out More

ONLINE

BAM! Body and Mind: Food and Nutrition
www.cdc.gov/bam/nutrition/index.html

Learn About Proteins
kidshealth.org/kid/nutrition/food/protein.html#cat119

MyPlate Kids' Place
www.choosemyplate.gov/kids

MyPlate: Protein Foods
www.choosemyplate.gov/food-groups/protein-foods.html

Nourish Interactive
www.nourishinteractive.com

IN BOOKS

Graimes, Nicola. *Kids' Fun and Healthy Cookbook.* New York: DK Publishing, 2007.

Royston, Angela. *Proteins for a Healthy Body.* Portsmouth, N.H.: Heinemann, 2009.

Royston, Angela. *Why We Need Proteins.* New York: Crabtree Publishing, 2011.

Schuh, Mari. *Protein on MyPlate.* North Mankato Minn.: Capstone Press, 2012.

Spilsbury, Louise. *Meat and Protein.* Portsmouth, N.H.: Heinemann, 2009.

Series Glossary of Key Terms

Carbohydrates: The types of molecules in food that we get most of our energy from. Foods like sugars and grains are especially high in carbohydrates.

Dairy: Milk or foods that are made from milk.

Diabetes: A disease where the body can't use sugar to produce energy correctly.

Diet: All the foods and nutrients that you normally eat.

Energy: The power stored in food that lets your body move around and carry out other body functions.

Farm: A place where plants and animals are grown and raised to produce food.

Fast food: Food designed to be ready for the customer as fast as possible. Usually it's more expensive and less healthy than fresh food, but it is very convenient.

Fiber: Tough parts of plant foods that your body can't digest. Fiber helps your digestive system function normally.

Fruits: A food group that includes the edible parts of plants that contain the seeds. They are often colorful and have a sweet flavor.

Grains: The seeds of various kinds of grass plant. Grains include rice, wheat, corn, and many others. They are high in carbohydrates and fiber, and can be stored for a long time.

Harvest: The process of gathering crops or the time when crops are gathered.

Local foods: Foods that are grown close to where they are eaten, so they don't have to be transported very far.

Minerals: Materials found naturally in metals or rocks. Our bodies need certain minerals in very small quantities.

Nutrients: Any part of food that our body uses in some way to survive and stay healthy.

Obesity: A state of being so overweight that it's bad for your health.

Organic: A way of producing food in which no genetic modifications, harmful pesticides, or hormones can be used.

Protein: The chemical parts of food that your body uses to build muscles and perform certain body processes. If your body runs out of carbohydrates and fat, it will start using protein for energy.

Vegetables: Plant foods that are usually made of the flower, stem, leaf, or root of a plant. They are usually high in fiber and certain nutrients.

Vitamins: Certain kinds of molecules that your body cannot produce. Instead, you need to get them in your diet to stay healthy.

Index

About the Author & Consultant

Celicia Scott lives in upstate New York. She worked in teaching before starting a second career as a writer.

Dr. Lisa Prock is a developmental behavioral pediatrician at Children's Hospital (Boston) and Harvard Medical School. She attended college at the University of Chicago, medical school at Columbia University, and received a master's degree in public health from the Harvard School of Public Health. Board-certified in general pediatrics and developmental behavioral pediatrics, she currently is Clinical Director of Developmental and Behavioral Pediatrics and Consultant to the Walker School, a residential school serving children in foster care. Dr. Prock has combined her clinical interests in child development and international health with advocacy for children in medical, residential, and educational settings since 1991. She has worked in Cambodia teaching pediatrics and studying tuberculosis epidemiology; and in Eastern Europe visiting children with severe neurodevelopmental challenges in orphanages. She has co-authored numerous original publications and articles for families. She is a also nonprofit board member for organizations and has received numerous local and national awards for her work with children and families.

Picture Credits